CONTENTS

HOW DO WE USE LETTERING?

How many different kinds of letters did you notice last time you came home? Next time, try counting them and notice how different they look. We see lettering all around us, giving us information, advertising the names of people and things, giving us instructions.

Signwriters paint signs using many different kinds of letters. Printers use different letters, called **typefaces**, for books, magazines and newspapers. Advertisers look for letters that will be bold and striking. We use handwriting to write letters to each other, and our writing is probably quite different when we put our names on books and folders.

▼ Many different styles of lettering have been used to attract attention to each of these advertisements.

▲ A signwriter painting letters with a brush and resting his hand on a *mahlstick* so that he doesn't smudge his work. Notice that he is holding his paint in his left hand.

VE
NG &
APHY

day

To Deanna, Alex, Jamie and Lizzie
and not forgetting Shelley (for
sitting on the work).

KINGFISHER
Kingfisher Publications Plc
New Penderel House, 283–288 High Holborn,
London WC1V 7HZ

First published in paperback by Kingfisher Publications Plc 1992
This edition published by Kingfisher Publications Plc 2000

2 4 6 8 10 9 7 5 3 1

1(TR)/1299/SC/HBM(FR)/128JAMA

Originally published in hardback by Kingfisher Publications Plc 1990

Text © Kingfisher Publications Plc 1990
Illustrations © Peter Halliday 1990

A CIP catalogue record for this book is available
from the British Library.

ISBN 0 86272 994 7

Edited by Annabel Warburg
Designed by Robert Wheeler
Illustrations by Peter Halliday
Cover Design by Mike Buckley
Phototypeset by Wyvern Typesetting, Bristol, England
Printed in Hong Kong

Photographic Acknowledgements

The publishers wish to thank the following for kindly
supplying photographs for this book:
Page 4 John Walmsley (*top*) The Hutchinson Library
(*bottom*); 5 Donald Jackson; 9 British Museum; 14 London
Transport Museum; 15 Victoria and Albert Museum; 18 Jenni
Grey and Designer Bookbinders; 22 Visual Arts Library;
26 British Library (*left*) Donald Jackson (*right*); 33 Visual Arts
Library; 37 Bennett, Lovatt & Associates Ltd; 38 British
Museum (*left*) Peter Clayton (*right*); 39 Visual Arts Library
(*left*) British Museum (*right*).

Picture Research: Elaine Willis

Author's Acknowledgements:
Adrian George, Michael Gullick, Donald Jackson,
Jen Lindsay, Brody Neuenschwander (illustration on
page 21), Bennett, Lovatt & Associates Ltd.

Pick up a magazine or newspaper and play 'Spot the Difference'. Choose a letter, perhaps your own initial, and find as many different versions as you can. Then work out what the differences are.

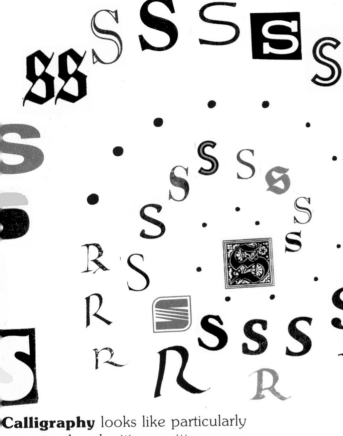

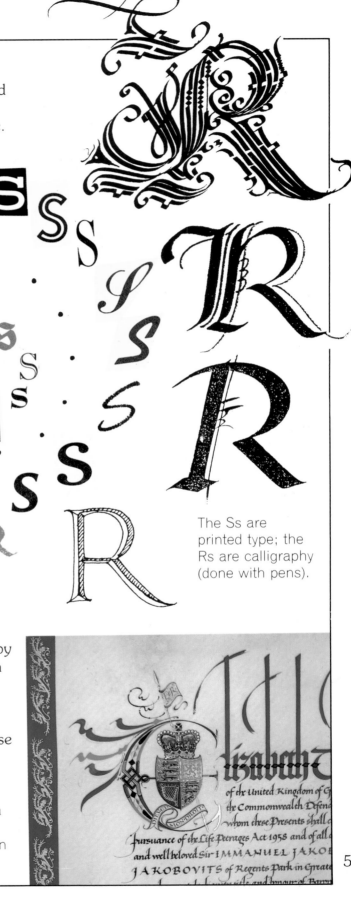

The Ss are printed type; the Rs are calligraphy (done with pens).

Calligraphy looks like particularly attractive handwriting, written very carefully. It is usually done using a pen or brush. Special documents, such as certificates and scrolls, may be written by a calligrapher. Calligraphers also design lettering for a printer to use or for a signwriter to copy. Calligraphers can make letters work in lots of different ways, to suit the subject and the purpose of what they are writing.

► Part of a scroll, called Royal Letters Patent, done by Donald Jackson, who is a scribe to the British Crown Office in the House of Lords. He made this hand-drawn copy of the original in 1988.

5

LETTERS AND PATTERNS

Letters make patterns make words.
To begin calligraphy you will need to practise writing patterns so that your letters are even.
Letters are pattern shapes. When we put these shapes together we can make words—our patterns then have meanings.

Try copying these patterns with a pencil or a fine felt-tipped pen. Make them as even as you can and try not to stop. If you do have to stop, lift your pencil or pen off the paper and then carefully re-start where you left off.

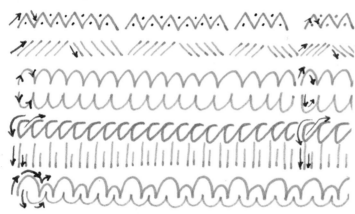

The arrows show the directions of the pen strokes.

(See page 37 for tips on holding pens if you are left-handed.)

When you can make really even patterns, try making patterns out of letters shaped like these below. You will notice that the patterns which you were making earlier are hidden inside the letter shapes.

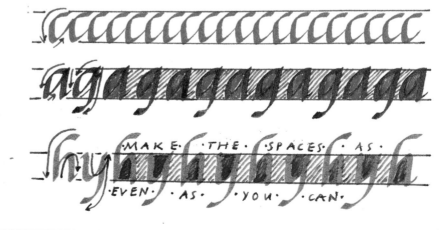

6

·S·H·E·L·L·E·Y·

With plenty of practice, you will find that you are able to make designs and pictures like the ones shown here. Copy the easy ones first and then try the bigger, more complicated ones. You will then be good enough to make up your own designs.

Hold your pen or pencil comfortably – don't grip it tightly – and make sure that you can see the tip without having to move your head to one side.

Some pens are made especially for calligraphy and have chisel-shaped tips like this . . .

HOLD THE PEN IN ONE POSITION FOR THIS

With tips like this you can make thick and thin strokes and make the patterns more varied. You can *see* straight away that pens like these give the letters more character. They make the spaces inside the letters more interesting too, so that they show through.

·USE· GUIDE· LINES· TO ·HELP·

7

ITALIC. Italic is a streamlined version of the Small Roman hand (see pages 14–15) and it was developed for use in the Italian chancery or legal offices at the same time that the Small Roman was becoming popular in Italy. It is sometimes called 'Chancery hand'. Modern italic type is similar to italic writing. 'Copperplate' handwriting is a later and modified form of italic from which our modern handwriting has developed.

" MAKE YOUR OWN CAPITALS "

ABCDEFGHIJKLMN

abcdefghijklmnopqrstuvwxyz

"CAPITALS ARE NO HIGHER THAN ASCENDERS"

ABCDEFGHIJ

& AMPERSAND = FROM LATIN ET = AND

x-height is about 5 nib widths

▶ A poem by John Donne written using italic calligraphy in ink and decorated using real fishing flies, paint and perspex (*plexiglas*) by Peter Halliday in 1982.

The Baite
by John Donne

Italic narrow sloping & flowing

Italic LETTERS ARE SQUEEZED NARROW

ABCDEFGHIJ

KLMNOPQRSTUVWXYZ

1234567890!?".

= NUMBERS CAN ASCEND & DESCEND = 1234567890"

=PEN ANGLE=
Your pen must always make the thin stroke in the same direction

only flourish where there is room

▶ A page from a volume presented to Henry VIII of England. It was written in the italic style in Italy in 1520.

PANDVLPHI COLLENVCII PISAVRENSIS APOLOGVS CVI TITVLVS AGENORIA

OPQRSTUVWXYZ

st hy e po

MOBILES AND DECORATIONS

You can make mobiles to hang from the ceiling or from shelves. The first mobiles that you make could just hang straight down, but you will probably soon want to be more adventurous and make mobiles like the one shown below.

MOBILES

You will need: shapes made out of paper or card, pens, a needle, thread, thin sticks or bits of twig or wire.

1. Decorate the paper shapes using patterns like the ones on pages six and seven.

2. Using the needle, make a hole at the top of each shape and use the thread to tie one shape to each end of a stick or piece of wire.

3. Find the point where the stick hangs level and tie a thread around the stick at this point. Tie the other end of the thread to one end of a second stick.

4. Tie a shape to the other end of the second twig so that it balances. Then keep adding more layers, adjusting the balance as the mobile gets bigger.

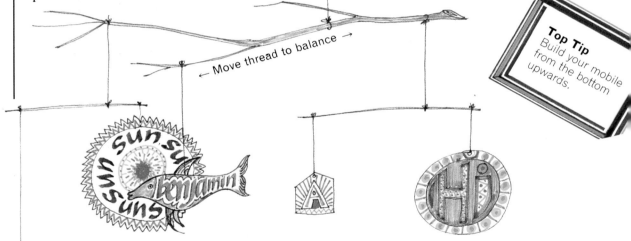

← Move thread to balance →

Top Tip
Build your mobile from the bottom upwards.

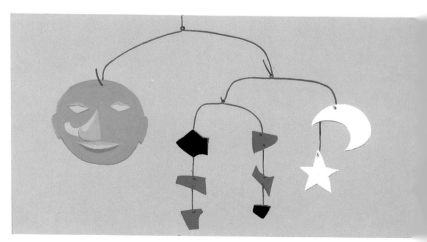

► Alexander Calder (1898–1976) was an American sculptor who made mobiles like this one.

TABLE DECORATIONS

You can write on almost any object that has a smooth surface. Some surfaces will be better if they are painted matt-white first, otherwise the ink from your pen may not show up properly. Find an everyday saying or a name and write with a felt-tipped pen in such a way that it makes an interesting design. You could fill in the spaces with patterns. Here are some ideas to try:

Look for smooth, roundish pebbles. Lightly draw your design in pencil first. Then work with felt-tipped pens or paints.

Make a tag or pendant out of a piece of wood. Ask an adult to drill a hole through the top.

Thread through

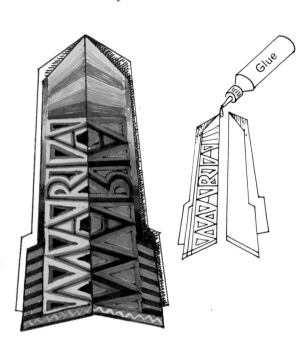

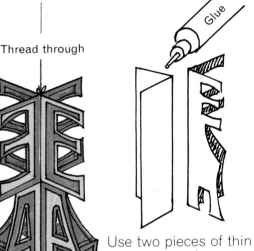

You can make standing decorations using thin card, glue and felt-tipped pens. Cut out and fold the card as shown in the illustration, then glue it onto a base made from stiff card.

Use two pieces of thin card 15cm × 9cm. Fold one piece and draw letters. Cut out and draw round it on the other piece. Cut out. Glue down back of fold. Decorate, thread and then hang up.

Make your own wrapping paper to wrap up presents or to cover presentation boxes or desk tidies. Use a large sheet of plain paper and decorate it with a design that you can repeat, using pens, crayons or pencils.

COLLAGES

As we have already seen, letters can be arranged as interlocking shapes. An attractive and decorative way of putting lots of letters together is to make a collage. You could also make a 'stained glass window' to hang up in your window.

A COLLAGE OF ONE LETTER

You will need: scissors, glue, magazines and newspapers, paper to stick the collage on to, pencils, felt-tipped pens.

We saw on page seven that there are lots of different styles and shapes of the same letter. Find some that are big enough to cut out easily (at least one centimetre in height). See how many different styles of the same letter you can find.

Look at the shapes at the endings of the letter strokes (called *serifs*): the differences in thickness and whether or not they slope.

To make a collage out of the letters, arrange them in the shape of the letter they represent and stick them down.

MORE COLLAGES

You can make attractive collages using lots of differing styles to spell out names. Always make sure that your design fits comfortably onto your paper before you start sticking it down.

MAKE A STAINED GLASS WINDOW

Here are two ways of making a collage into a stained glass window. When you hold them up, the light will shine through the tissue or tracing paper.

Charlie

Contrast the lettering and make some lively and amusing labels.

You will need: sheets of black paper, tracing paper for **A**, coloured tissue paper for **B**, glue, a black felt-tipped pen or marker pen, a small pointed pair of scissors.

WINDOW A

1. Cut a hole in a piece of black paper.
2. Cut a piece of tracing paper that is smaller than the black paper but big enough to cover the hole. Glue the two pieces of paper together.
3. Design a collage that will fit into the hole; draw it onto another sheet of black paper. Cut out the design and stick it onto the tracing paper.
4. To make your collage look like pieces of stained glass, draw in some lines on the tracing paper using a black pen. Colour in the pieces of 'glass'.

WINDOW B

1. Draw a design onto a piece of black paper, leaving a margin of about two centimetres all the way around your design. Make sure that all the details in the design touch either another detail or the outer margin.
2. Carefully cut out the spaces in between the details in the design.
3. On the back of the design, stick pieces of coloured tissue paper across the spaces you have cut out.
4. Draw any extra details you want onto the tissue paper using a black pen.

A

B

13

abcdefghijklmnopqrstuv

LOOK AT THE SIZE OF THE 'COUNTER' TO WORK OUT HOW LARGE TO WRITE!

◄ The London Underground map lettering was designed by Edward Johnston in 1916, based on his studies of Carolingian and Humanistic calligraphy.

Journey planner

ABCDEFGHIJKLMNO

New York

London ~ Paris

Lucie ~ Alice

Benjamin

14

ROMAN LETTER
1st Century AD

SMALL ROMAN
or Bookhand

▶ A page from a book, written and decorated in Italy around 1500, in the Humanistic style. Notice the Roman capitals, both written and painted, and the clear simplicity of the writing The book is called the Bentivoglio Hours.
(V & A Museum Reid MS 64.)

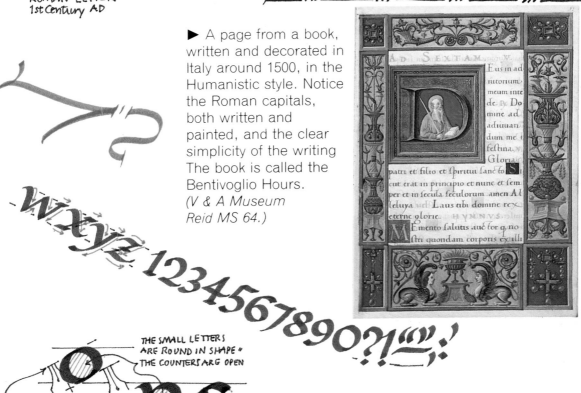

wxyz 1234567890?!:;

THE SMALL LETTERS ARE ROUND IN SHAPE & THE COUNTERS ARE OPEN

O ns

KEEP PEN AT THIS ANGLE

Caspar · Stephanie

PQRSTUVWXYZ

& & &
Ampersands

MAKE THE CAPITALS QUITE SMALL

Charlie Chaplin

MAKE YOUR OWN BOOK

Making your own book is not as difficult as you might imagine. A book is only a number of sheets of paper joined together in order.
Here are some ideas for making simple books.

MAKING A ZIGZAG BOOK

You will need: a piece of A4 paper (21 cm by 30 cm); pencil; ruler; scissors; glue; pens; thin card or stiff paper.

1. Fold the paper lengthways and cut it in half.

2. Fold each half of paper into a zigzag of four. Join the two zigzags together by gluing a narrow strip at the back of each zigzag edge. You will then have a zigzag book which has eight sides.

3. Fold the zigzag together. Make a cover by sticking some card or stiff paper on each end.

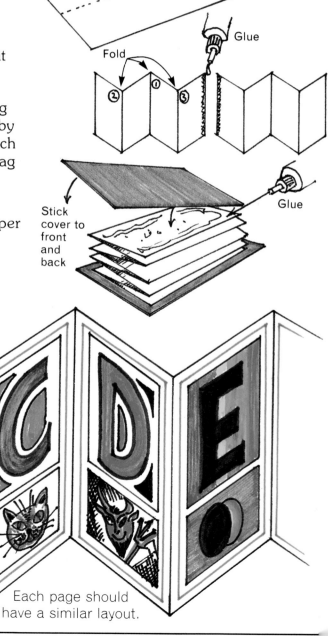

Cut paper in half

Fold

Glue

Stick cover to front and back

Glue

Each page should have a similar layout.

◀ You can decorate the margins.

▲ Leave a margin all the way around each page, as shown above. The lower margin should be wider than the others. The space inside the margins is called the text area. Put all your writing and design inside this area.

4. When you have decided on the subject matter, put your designs on the pages.

Some ideas for subject matter:
– put one letter of your name on each page and use some of your patterns from pages six and seven as a frame
– find a poem and fit a verse onto each page
– put a picture on the left-hand page and some writing on the page opposite

Top Tip
Use small amounts of glue and wait for it to stick.

Top Tip
Don't forget that you can use both sides of the book.

MAKE A SINGLE SECTION BOOK

The writing and illustrations in handmade books are usually all completed before the pages are sewn together, but here you can make the book first and then decide what to put into it.

You will need: three sheets of A4 paper (21 cm by 30 cm); one sheet of coloured stiff A3 paper or thin card (42 cm by 30 cm), folded in half for the cover; a piece of embroidery thead (or similar); a needle; a ruler; a pencil; pens; paints or crayons for decorating (optional).

1. Fold each sheet of paper in half across the width and slip the sheets into each other; slip the paper into the folded stiff paper or card that you have chosen for the cover.

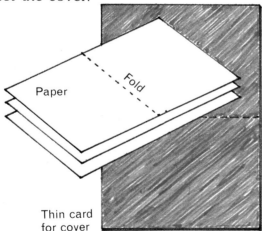

Paper

Fold

Thin card for cover

2. Keeping the pages and cover together, measure halfway down the inside fold (called the 'gutter'), mark and make a hole with a needle through all the sheets of paper and card. Make sure it is exactly in the fold. Make two more marks in the gutter, one between the centre and the top and one between the centre and the bottom. Using the needle, make holes through these marks.

▲ A hand-bound book, called a 'fine binding'. The flat box behind the book is a slipcase, used to protect the book. This fine binding was made by Jenni Grey.

Slip each folded page inside the others

Top Tip
It is a good idea to make a 'mock-up' book to try out your ideas.

3. Following the diagrams carefully, sew the thread through the gutter. Make sure that you start on the inside and take the thread through to the outside. Finish by sewing the thread through the hole where you started, back to the inside.

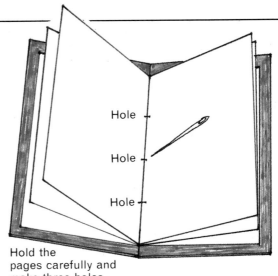

Hold the pages carefully and make three holes.

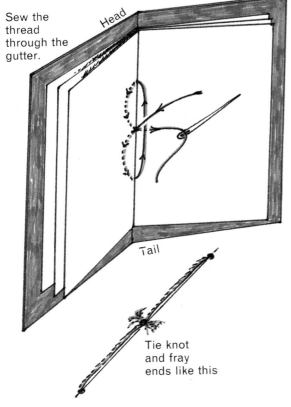

Sew the thread through the gutter.

Head

Tail

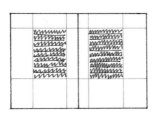

Tie knot and fray ends like this

4. Tie a neat knot over the long thread which runs down the gutter. Cut the thread about one centimetre from the knot and fray the ends out with the point of the needle so that the knot cannot come undone.

5. Draw your ideas for designs on some practice paper. Follow the diagram below showing the size of the margins and mark out guide lines lightly on each page. Put your design into the book.

Page plan

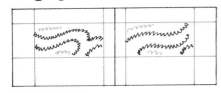

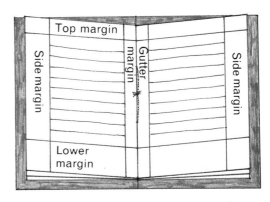

Top margin

Side margin

Gutter margin

Side margin

Lower margin

(The gutter margin should be the same size as the side margins but split on either side of the fold.)

▲ If your text is short, use wider margins to make it fit centrally on the page.

6. If you want to make a longer book, you can add extra sheets of A4 paper before you sew it together. Each sheet, folded, adds four more pages.

GOTHIC OR BLACKLETTER. This developed in the countries of northern Europe from about 1200 and was used until the 1500s when books began to be printed rather than hand-written. The reason it is called 'Blackletter' is that the heavy black letters are so closely spaced that the pages of writing look black. The first printed book was printed in this style by Johannes Gutenburg in Germany in 1450.

abcdefghijklmn

ABCDEFG
OPQRST

USE PEN EDGEWAYS

DRAW GUIDE LINES AND MARK OUT BEFORE MAK-ING PATTERN

TWO PEN STROKES

Bilbo

Roger

Peter Roma Claire

20

Gothic
or Blackletter

BUILD UP PATTERNS BIT BY BIT

▲ Part of a poem by John Donne, written in the gothic style by Brody Neuenschwander in 1989. This is his design version done in ink on top of bronze powder paint.

HIJKLMN
UVWXYZ

KEEP PEN ANGLE THE SAME ALWAYS

opqrstuvwxyz

MAKE THIN LINES BY TURNING ON ITS CORNER

IF YOU WANT TO WRITE LIKE THIS YOU MUST PRACTICE LIKE THIS

Calligraphy

SCROLL AND CASE

*The earliest books were made by the Ancient Egyptians almost 4500 years ago. They were written on **scrolls** — long strips of a paper made from a reed called papyrus, which were stored rolled up around a stick. Even today, some documents and certificates are written on special paper or parchment and made into scrolls.*

MAKING A SCROLL AND CASE

You will need: stiff paper (A4 or 21 cm by 30 cm); a length of ribbon about 26 cm long; a cardboard tube about 30 cm long; thin card measuring 6 cm by 20 cm; a pencil; a ruler; scissors; glue; pens; a strip of thin wood or thick card 21 cm long; sandpaper; paper for covering the scroll case (optional).

▼ A scroll with the seal still attached. It was written for King Richard the First of England in 1194. As a legal document, the bottom was folded up to the last line of writing and then the ribbon was threaded through so that nothing could be added afterwards without breaking the seal.

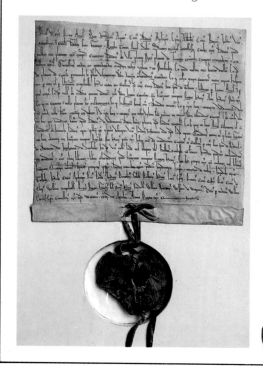

1. Design some showy flourishes for the top of the scroll, but do lots of practice first so that you can get them right.

2. Write out the message clearly and attractively, leaving a space of about three centimetres at the bottom of the scroll.

3. Fold the bottom of the scroll over the thin strip of wood or thick card.

4. Tie the ribbon as shown in the illustration.

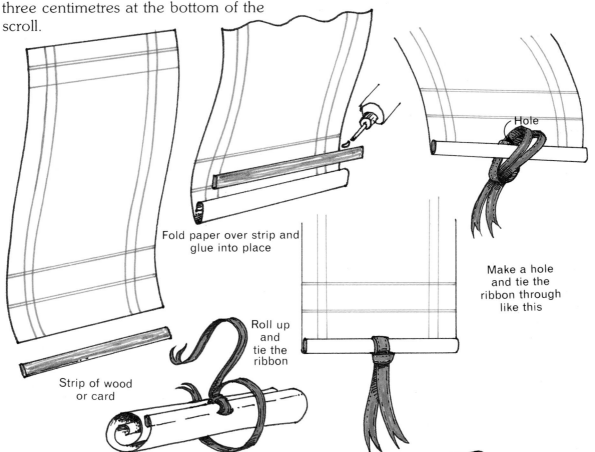

Fold paper over strip and glue into place

Strip of wood or card

Roll up and tie the ribbon

Hole

Make a hole and tie the ribbon through like this

5. To make the case, ask an adult to cut off about seven centimetres of the cardboard tube. With fine sandpaper, smooth off the rough edges. Roll up the strip of thin card and glue it into the top of the long tube, leaving about four centimetres sticking out. The short piece of the tube will fit over the card as a lid for your case.

You can decorate the case by covering it with wrapping paper. (See page 11 for instructions on how to make your own wrapping paper).

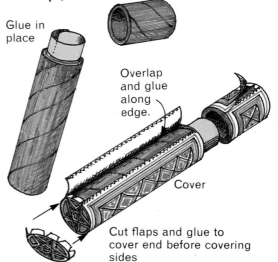

Glue in place

Overlap and glue along edge.

Cover

Cut flaps and glue to cover end before covering sides

23

SIMPLE LAYOUTS

Making a design to go on to such things as birthday cards, gift tags and labels needs a little planning to make it fit properly and look as you would like. It is easiest to make a rough design first, called a 'layout'. You can 'lay out' your idea on paper in such a way that you can scribble over it to change and improve it.

You will need: practice paper; thin card or stiff paper; pencil; pens; glue; scissors.

When you plan a design, you may find that part of it is all right but that you want to change the rest. Rather than re-doing the whole design, you can make your changes on another sheet of paper (be sure that the paper is the right size). You can then cut the new piece out and paste it in position on your original design.

When you are satisfied with the whole design (you can cut out and paste as much as you like), you will have what is called a 'paste-up', which is a complete design that you can copy or trace.

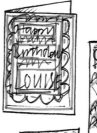

Start with small rough sketches of the layout

When you have experimented with your rough layout until you are happy with it, you can copy your final design onto card or paper.

Concertina cards

Don't be too disappointed if you can't get things right at first: you will get better with practice.

CUT

FOLD

MICHAEL

MICHAEL

Place names

Charlotte

GREETINGS

Noël

Thanks

Gift tags

Party

NEXT SATURDAY

8-till LATE

RSVP

YES I can come
SORRY - can't come

Party invitation

M!

Decoration

MEMBERSHIP CARD

H CLUB 4

Membership card

FOR JANE

NOEL

Card

feliz navidad

DECORATING INITIALS

A clever way of using letters is to decorate or 'illuminate' them. There are lots of ways of decorating letters—look at signs and advertisements to get some good ideas.

You can start by making a design on some paper and colouring it in. Always make sure that the letter shape shows clearly. If you make the decoration too complicated, the letter will be difficult to recognize.

◀ In the days before books were printed, special books had initials which were highly decorated. They were often 'illuminated' by having shining gold leaf for the letter or background. This letter 'H' is from a 12th century manuscript.

▲ A page from a sampler of initials and heraldic devices painted and illuminated by Donald Jackson in 1988.

DRAW IN THE OUTLINE FIRST

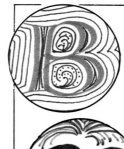

MAKE A BUTTON BADGE

Make a button badge using thick card. Stick a safety pin to the back using sticky tape.

Build up multi-stroke letters bit by bit. Make sure that the gap in between is even.

DESIGNING MONOGRAMS

A monogram is a design linking together two or more letters (for example, your initials). A monogram can be used just for decoration, or for putting on a letterhead, or to put on stickers for labelling your things. Draw several ideas lightly in pencil first, to find the best one. It is a good idea to make the initials weave in and out of each other, or to join and merge letters.

Design your own coat of arms.

PLH

Versal letter P

DESIGN USING 'S' AND 'O'

Versals were originally used at the beginning of a verse or paragraph.

27

WORD PICTURES

*We have already seen how to make patterns from letters and create words (pages six and seven). Words can also be made into patterns and pictures. These are called **calligrams**.*

There are many ways of making calligrams. First, try some simple ideas like those shown here. Some are made from letters only, not words. You can make them by repeating the same words and fitting them into the shape representing the subject of the word. You can even write short descriptions or poems.

1. Scribble out your idea in pencil (use pencil so that you can make changes by erasing and working over).
2. When you have worked out your idea, draw just the outline, in pencil again, then start writing with the pen.
3. You may want to change the size of your pen or try out different colours.

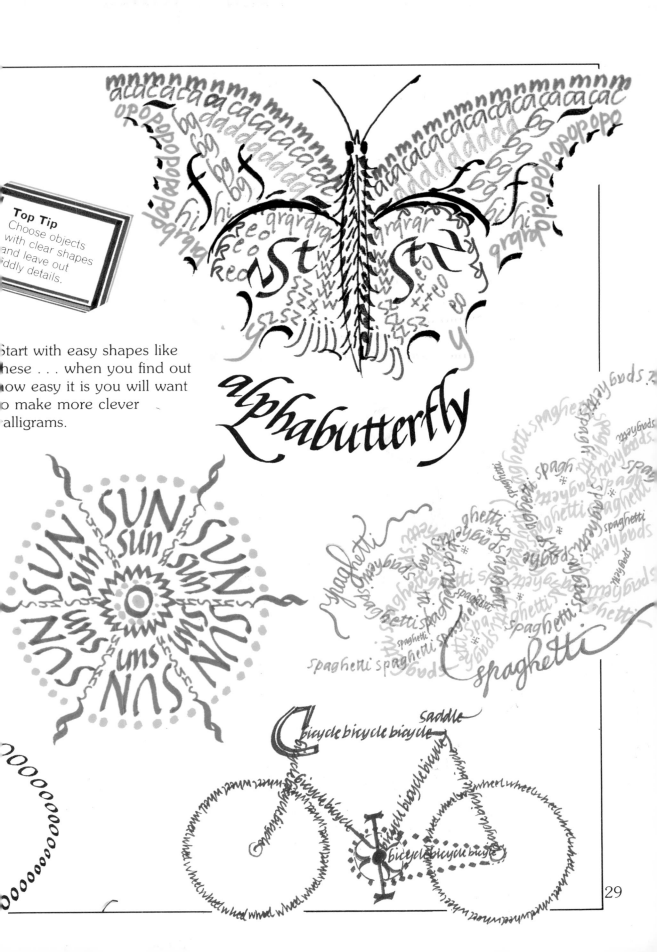

29

Top Tip
Choose objects with clear shapes and leave out fiddly details.

Start with easy shapes like these . . . when you find out how easy it is you will want to make more clever calligrams.

alphabutterfly

SUN

spaghetti

bicycle

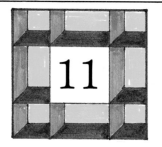

GRAPHICS-1

Calligraphy and lettering can be attractive and decorative but there are many useful things that you can make too. Why not impress your friends by making your own letter-head, membership card or your own tape cassette insert?

MAKING A TAPE CASSETTE INSERT

You will need: Cassette case; cassette insert (to draw around); practice paper; thin card or stiff paper; pencil; ruler; scissors; pens; glue.

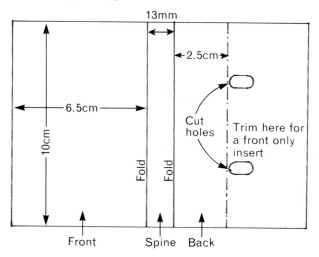

1. Find a cassette insert and draw around it on the thin card or paper to make a shape to put your design on.

Try out some rough designs in colour to get a good idea of how your cassette insert will look.

2. Try out three or four designs, in rough first, on the practice paper. Colour them in roughly. Cut and fold them to size and see what they look like in the case.

3. Select the best design and draw it out on the card carefully and lightly in pencil. Colour your design in. This can be your final version or a final rough (sometimes called a visual). Fold it and put it into the cassette case.

Look at the ideas illustrated here and decorate some writing paper with your own letter-head. Turn to pages 26 and 27 for some more ideas for ways of decorating your initials.

Top Tip
You could try using typeface letters from your collage designs on pages 12 and 13.

172 Main Street Anytown
Tel 123·456·789

HARRY ZEITGEIST

Top Tip
Use the cut and paste techniques described on pages 22 and 23.

Invitation

COME TO THE CONCERT

Invitation   Invitation

If you have access to a photocopier, do your designs in black or in pencil outline so that you can do several copies and then colour them in by hand.

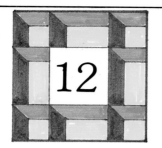

GRAPHICS-2

Some of the most dramatic use of lettering has been on posters and in advertising. Often the designers combine lettering with pictures, but sometimes printers use lots of different type which creates an amazing variety of patterns.

Making Dramatic Use of Letters

When making posters and advertisements, you need good ideas to get your message across, clear and well-chosen letter forms, and a well-organized design. Work out your idea in an order of priorities like this:

● What has your poster got to do?— (advertise a disco, dance, school play?).
● What is the most important part of your message? Work out an order of importance (eg. what, when, where, how much, etc).

● Think of a bold picture or pattern which is relevant to the event and will attract attention.

When designing a poster, start by making a few rough 'thumb-nail' sketches, then choose the best one to work on at full size. Follow the cut and paste techniques for the original layout, as described on pages 22 and 23.

 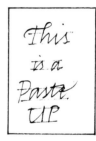

Start with thumb-nail sketches.

This is a PASTE UP

Try out the lettering you have chosen.

Draw some rules and do some careful versions of the lettering.

Select the best letters and paste them down. Check the spacing between the letters and words.

◀ Designers of book jackets often try to use lettering to suit the subject of the book.

The technique used for designing posters can be used for anything where visual impact is important: advertising, book jackets or package design.

Designers often get inspiration from all kinds of different sources, so keep looking out for new ideas. You could start to keep a scrapbook of examples of lettering you find striking and interesting. It is also a good idea to keep a sketchbook, so that you can make small, rough sketches.

Perspective

▲ Throughout the 20th century, artists and designers have used lettering and painting in creative ways in posters like this one by E. Heckel.

Make all lines join at the vanishing point.

The farther away you put the vanishing point, the more you appear to be looking up (or down) at the word.

Vanishing point

Vanishing point

Lettering on a curve

Cut out each letter.

1. Draw the lettering in a straight line and cut out each letter.
2. Using a pair of compasses, draw two lines as a guide. The distance between the lines should be the same as the height of the letters.
3. Lay down the letters, check the spacing and paste in position.
4. Copy or trace for use on the final version.

Draw guide lines using compasses. The distance between them should be the height of the letters.

MAKING PENS

Have you noticed the number of different pens it is possible to buy? Next time you go to a stationers, you will probably see lots: ball-points, felt-tips, cartridge pens, roller-points . . . The prices vary greatly too.

Until about 150 years ago, making a pen would have been something that all children at schools would have learnt to do. The only pens available were **quills**, which were made from feathers. Being able to cut and sharpen a quill-pen with a penknife was a basic skill. Some calligraphers still use quills today because they feel that they are better for certain special pieces of calligraphy.

With a fine pointed brush you can paint fine lines by just touching the paper with the tip, or you can thicken the stroke by pressing harder and you can move the brush sideways. Experiment and try out various paints and colours. The flat, one stroke brushes can be used in the same way as a pen, but if you press a little harder the stroke will be thicker.

Quill pen
Quills must be treated to harden them and are best when cut by an expert using a quill knife.

Side view   Below

Almost anything that is strong enough and is shaped like a narrow tube can be made into a pen. The important thing is the shape of the nib. Ask an adult to help you cut the end of the tube into the shape illustrated here for the reed pen (*below*). To write with your pen, dip the nib into fountain pen ink.

Reed pen
Must be cut with a sharp knife to this shape (ask an adult to help).

Below
Side view

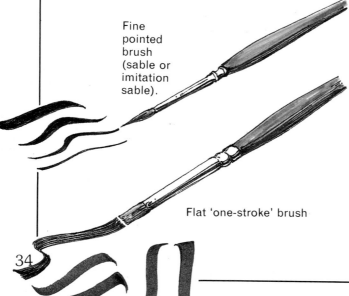

Fine pointed brush (sable or imitation sable).

Flat 'one-stroke' brush

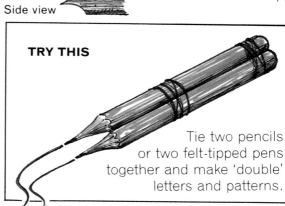

TRY THIS

Tie two pencils or two felt-tipped pens together and make 'double' letters and patterns.

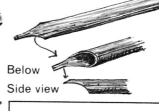

MAKING YOUR OWN FELT PEN

You will need: a bulldog clip; polystyrene; thin felt or a piece of old blanket or a piece of wadding (such as that used for anoraks); scissors.

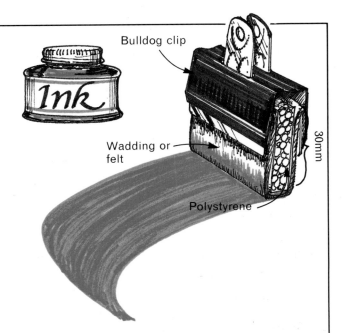

1. Cut a piece of polystyrene to the width of the bulldog clip and about 30 millimetres in length.

2. Cut a piece of felt, blanket or wadding to the same width as the polystyrene and about 70 millimetres in length.

3. Cover the polystyrene with the felt or wadding and put them together into the bulldog clip, making sure that the covering is pulled tight.

The pen can be dipped into fountain pen ink and can be used on lining paper (used under wallpaper) or on large pieces of drawing paper. Although these pens are for quite large writing, you will find them fun to play around with and useful for posters. Be careful to have plenty of newspaper underneath.

FABRIC PAINTS AND DYES

Some crayons and felt-tipped pens and paints are specially made for drawing on fabrics. Use them to decorate tee-shirts or scarves. You can either draw directly onto the fabric or you can cut some templates and stencils first. Plan your design before you start – you can't make corrections! If you want to work on a tee-shirt, put some stiff card inside (to protect the back) and tape it onto a flat board. Outline your design with soft pencil and make sure that you follow the instructions for using the paints properly. Hold the area where you are working quite tightly because fabric stretches when you work on it.

PENS, PAPERS, INKS, PAINTS

The information here is only a rough guide to the many different kinds of pens and supplies available. You may find a number of other types of pen. Try them out before you buy so that you make sure you get what you want.

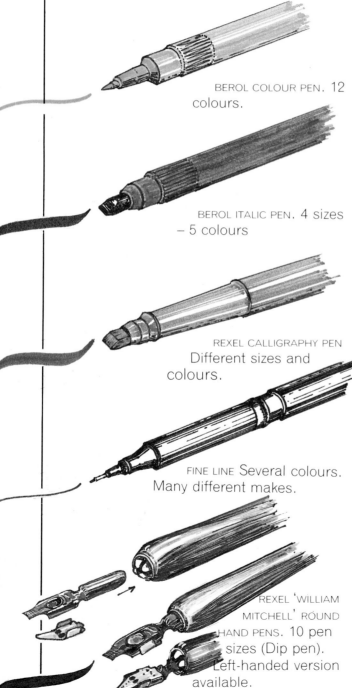

BEROL COLOUR PEN. 12 colours.

BEROL ITALIC PEN. 4 sizes – 5 colours

REXEL CALLIGRAPHY PEN Different sizes and colours.

FINE LINE Several colours. Many different makes.

REXEL 'WILLIAM MITCHELL' ROUND HAND PENS. 10 pen sizes (Dip pen). Left-handed version available.

PENS

Felt-tipped and fibre tip pens

cannot be refilled. Choose ones that are waterproof. **Cartridge pens** can be refilled by replacing the empty cartridge with a full one. Some are supplied with a refillable cartridge which can be filled with coloured ink. Never use waterproof ink in a cartridge pen and wash it thoroughly after changing the colour. To use a **dip pen** use ink in bottles, preferably non-waterproof. Dip just the tip into the ink. Have a paint rag or a kitchen tissue handy to wipe the pen. Always wash the pen after use.

PAPERS

Most art shops will have a selection of pads and papers. Smooth writing paper or smooth drawing paper is suitable for calligraphy. Layout pads are useful because the paper is thin, so that you can see through it to work over designs in order to copy or change them. The paper also takes ink and colour well. Coloured 'cover' papers can be used and they will take ink or colours.

INKS AND PAINTS

The best kind of ink for calligraphy is one that is non-waterproof. Any ink for use in cartridge pens will be good for practice, but for best results get some calligraphy ink. The finest black inks are Chinese or Japanese inks which often come in the form of short sticks and have to be ground with water. They can also be bought in liquid form. For

▲ The author at work.

drawing and outlining use either a fineline felt-tipped pen or waterproof drawing ink.
Your local art shop will have many different kinds of paints. Use watercolours, either in tubes such as designer's gouache, or in small pans as in painting sets.

IF YOU ARE LEFT-HANDED, follow the illustration below as a guide to holding your calligraphy and italic pens to make the thick and thin strokes at the proper angle. Turn your paper at an angle; move the paper slightly to the left and turn your wrist so that the edge of the pen makes the thin stroke at an angle of 45° to the line.

Position yourself and your work so that you can see what you have written. It helps to use a board which you can lean on at a slope against the work table.

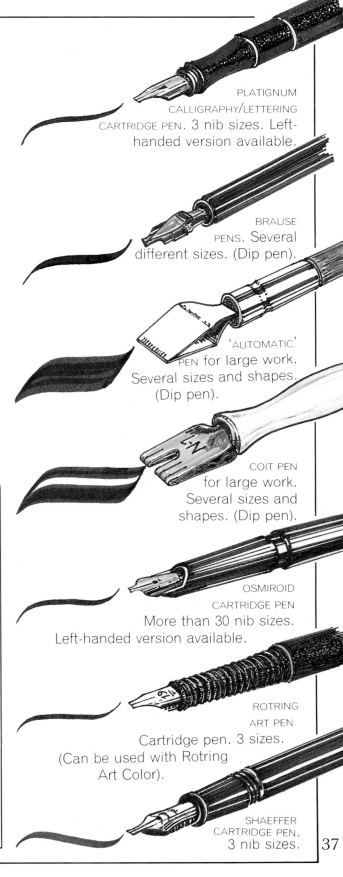

PLATIGNUM CALLIGRAPHY/LETTERING CARTRIDGE PEN. 3 nib sizes. Left-handed version available.

BRAUSE PENS. Several different sizes. (Dip pen).

'AUTOMATIC' PEN for large work. Several sizes and shapes. (Dip pen).

COIT PEN for large work. Several sizes and shapes. (Dip pen).

OSMIROID CARTRIDGE PEN More than 30 nib sizes. Left-handed version available.

ROTRING ART PEN Cartridge pen. 3 sizes. (Can be used with Rotring Art Color).

SHAEFFER CARTRIDGE PEN. 3 nib sizes.

HISTORY OF WRITING

The way that we use calligraphy, lettering and printing today is the result of many centuries of change. All writing and lettering came originally from the use of pictures to record information. We can still see examples of how prehistoric people painted pictures on cave walls to describe their hunting.

The most famous kind of picture writing is Egyptian hieroglyphic, meaning 'sacred carved inscription', first used about 5000 years ago. The idea of writing spread through different civilizations in the eastern Mediterranean. As the pictures were adapted for different languages or written using different tools, they became more streamlined and eventually changed into letters.

	m	f	p	b	w	vowel sound does not exist in English
z or s	s	ch or sh	ch	h	h	r
dj	d	th	t	g	k	q

Hieroglyphs and their approximate sound

An Egyptian scribe

◀ Many Roman tablets and inscriptions survive today. We think that the letters were first painted with a flat brush and then 'incised' by carving with a chisel to preserve them.

▲ The most important difference between hieroglyphs and earlier writing is that each picture represents a *sound*.

The Greeks were the first to use letters that we recognize today. They passed their letters on to the Romans, who developed the alphabet which we are familiar with today. They used only capital letters.

◀ Modern lettering artists still study Roman Inscriptions today to improve their understanding of letters.

Sometimes they were filled with lead or bronze.

38

Cuneiform c.4000BC   Stylus marks   Egyptian Hieroglyphics 3100BC- AD 400   Phoenician c.700BC   Classical Greek 500BC

riting on a soft
ay tablet using
stylus.

Parchment (specially treated animal skin)
radually replaced earlier writing
urfaces, such as papyrus and clay
ablets. By AD 100, a method had been
eveloped of folding sheets of
archment-papyrus and sewing them
ogether to make a book. During the late
'00s, the scholar Alcuin of York
eveloped a style of writing that made
ooks easier to plan and to read.
Capitals were used for headings and
mall letters, or 'half unicals' were used
or the main text. Books were made by
and until about 1500.

▲ Here a scribe is teaching his pupil. He
has a special chair with a board fixed to it;
the ink well is placed in a hole on the
board. He writes with a quill pen and is
holding the parchment down with the tip of
his pen knife (used to sharpen his pen).

In about 1450 a German named
Johannes Gutenberg invented a method
of printing using separate pieces of metal
for each letter that could be arranged in
any combination. This made it possible
to produce many copies of the same
book and the metal, or type could be
used again. Until the early years of the
20th century, printing methods changed
very little, although the machinery used
became much more advanced. Since the
1950s, the development of *off-set litho
printing* and advances in micro-
computers have revolutionized printing
methods.

◀ A page from a
book printed by
the Venetian
Aldus Manutius in
1499. He produced
beautiful books in
small and
inexpensive
volumes.

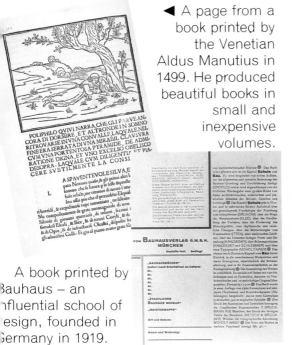

A book printed by
Bauhaus – an
nfluential school of
esign, founded in
Germany in 1919.

Calligraphy *Calligraphy*
Calligraphy

▲ The most modern way of printing is to
use a laser printer. This will print quickly
and accurately and in any shape or style
you choose.

INDEX